Mandalas
FOR MINDFULNESS

igloobooks

igloobooks

Published in 2016
by Igloo Books Ltd
Cottage Farm
Sywell
NN6 0BJ
www.igloobooks.com

Cover designed by Lee Italiano
Designed by Stephen Jorgensen
Edited by Vicky Taylor

Front and back covers and interiors illustrated by Ashish Dhir
All other images: iStock

FIR003 0116
2 4 6 8 10 9 7 5 3 1
ISBN: 978-1-78557-848-9

Printed and manufactured in China

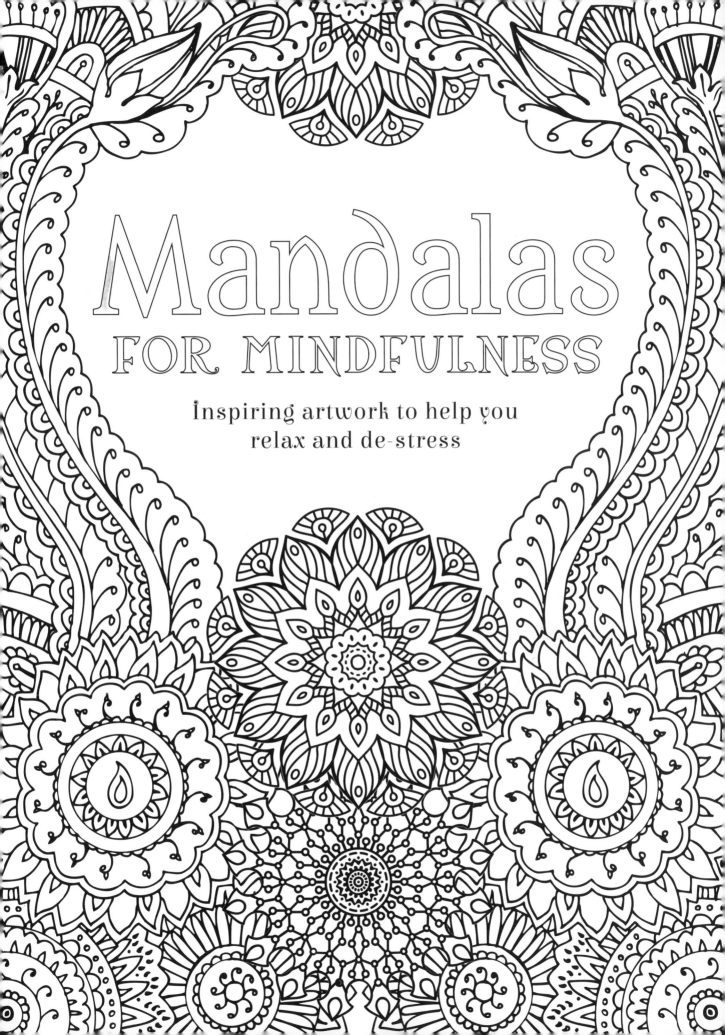

Mandalas
FOR MINDFULNESS

Inspiring artwork to help you
relax and de-stress

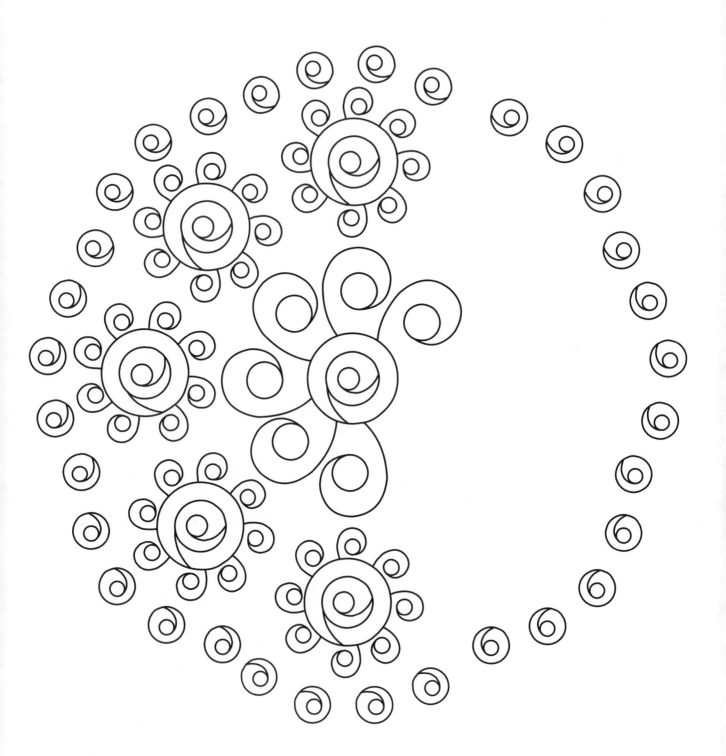

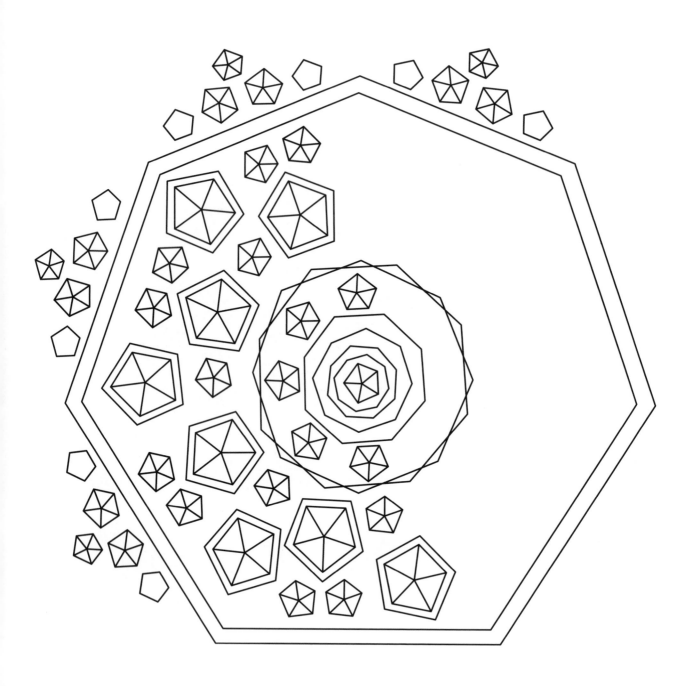

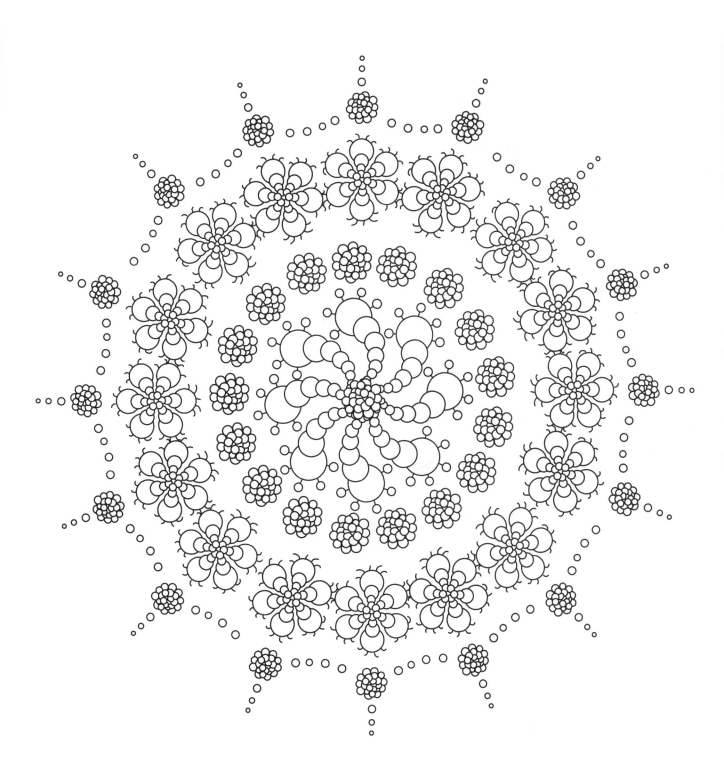

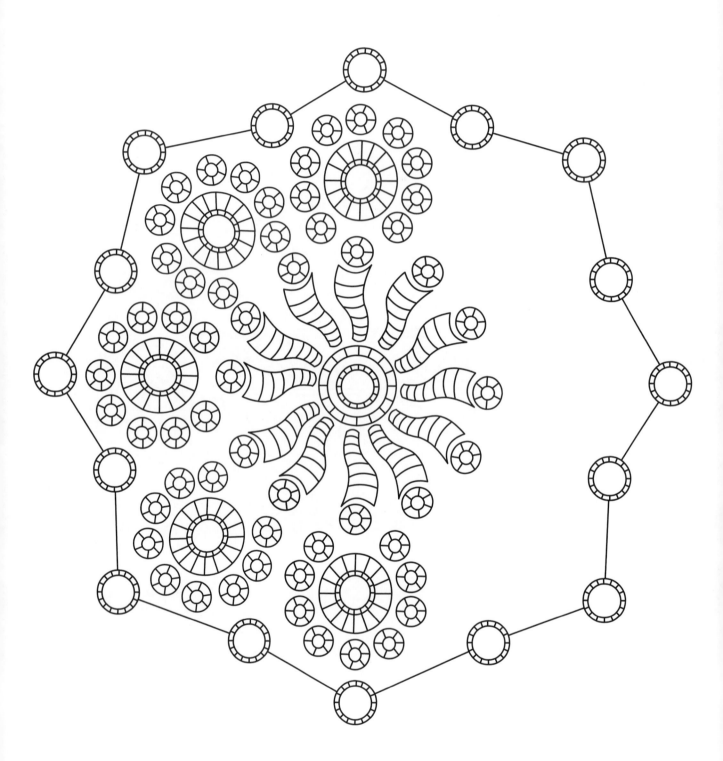

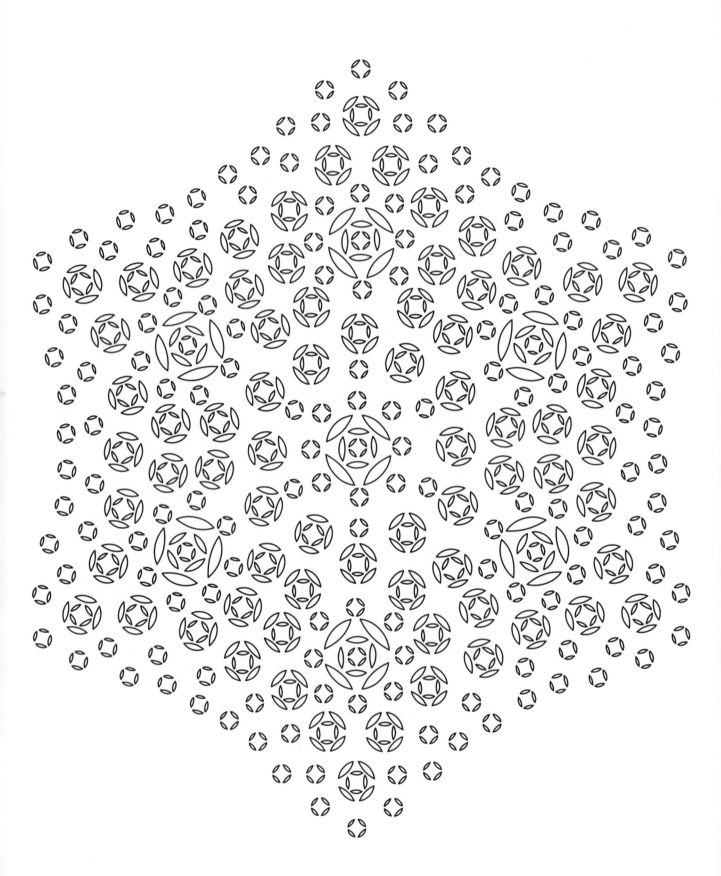

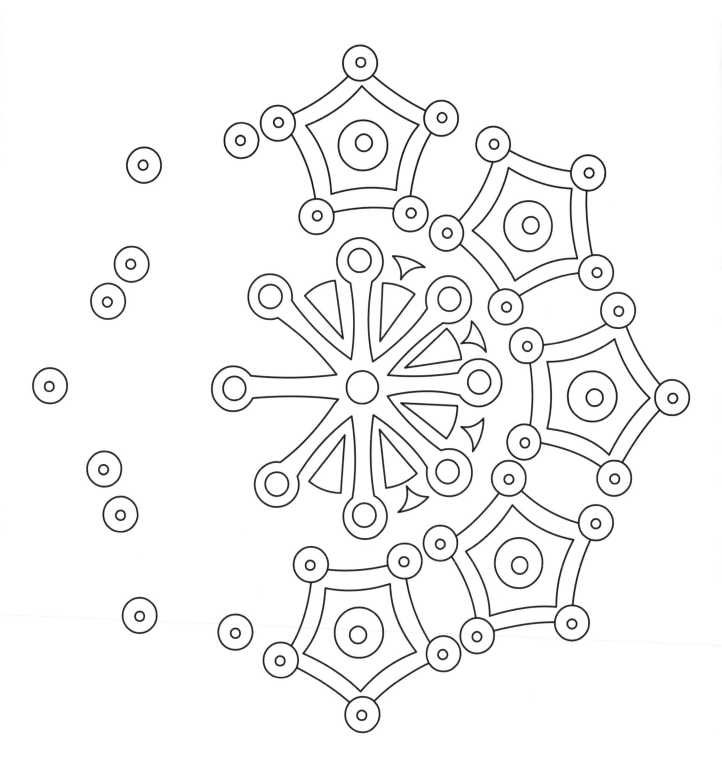

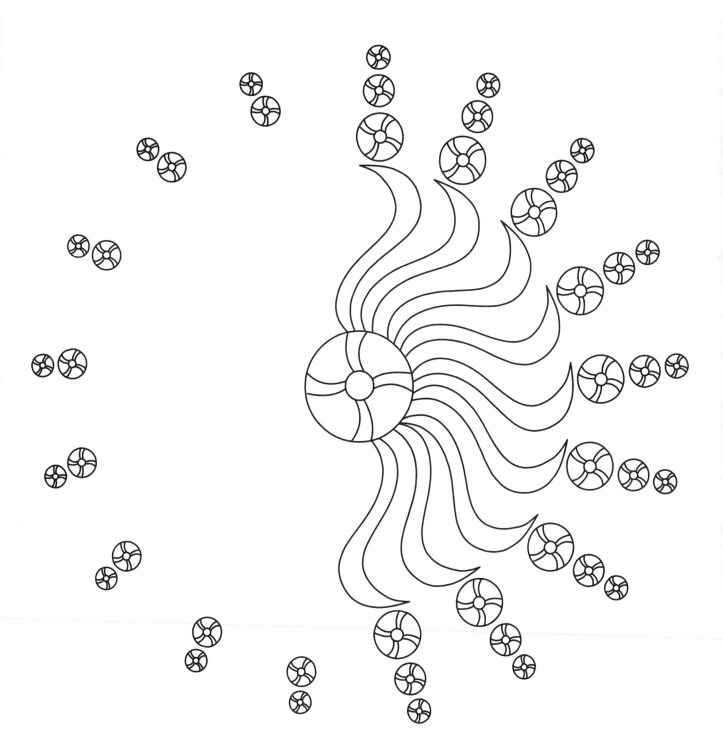

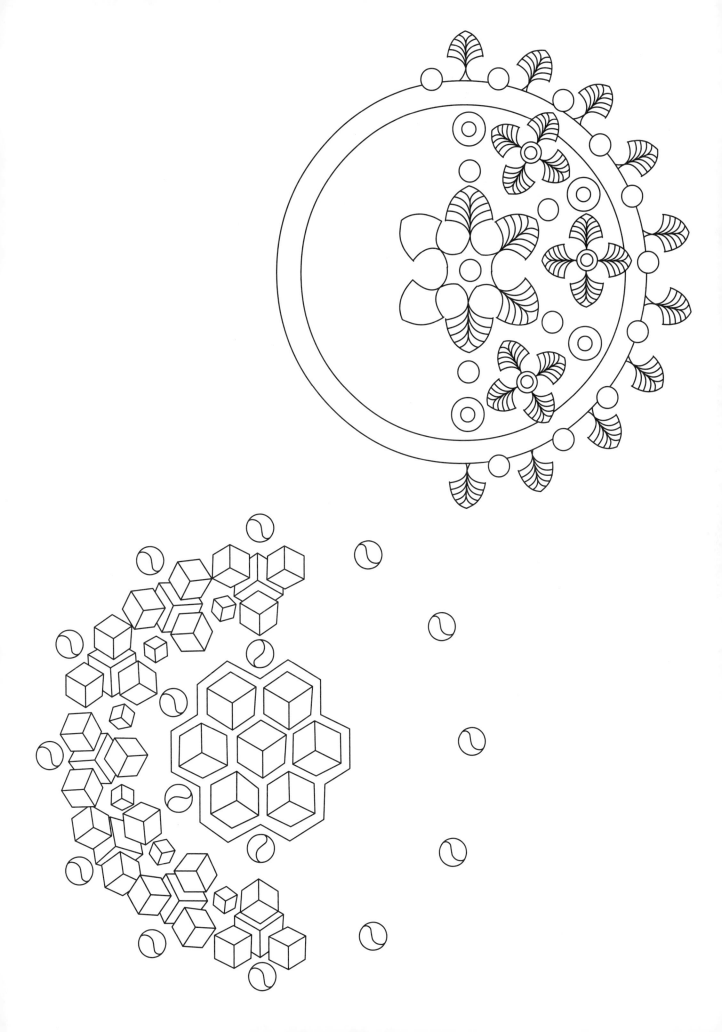

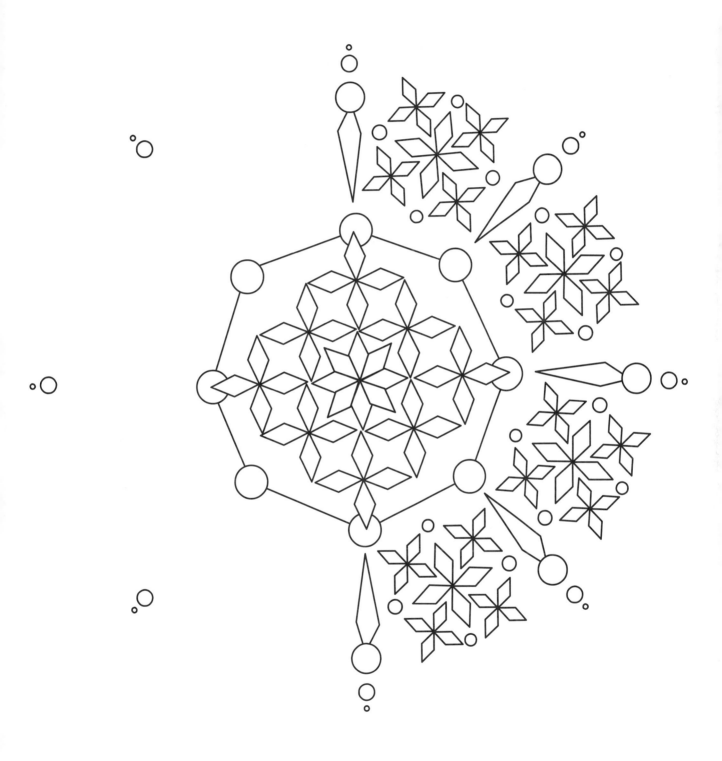

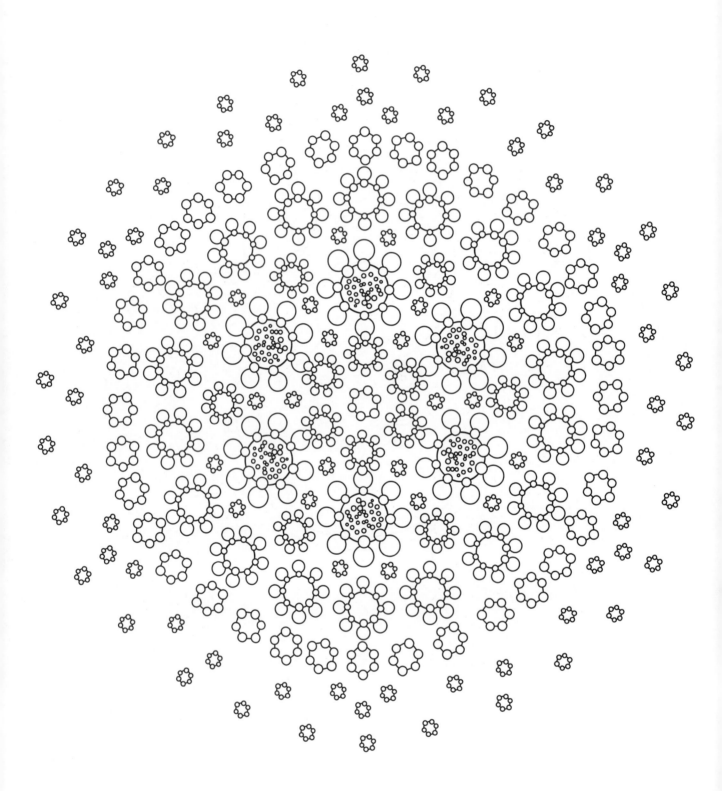

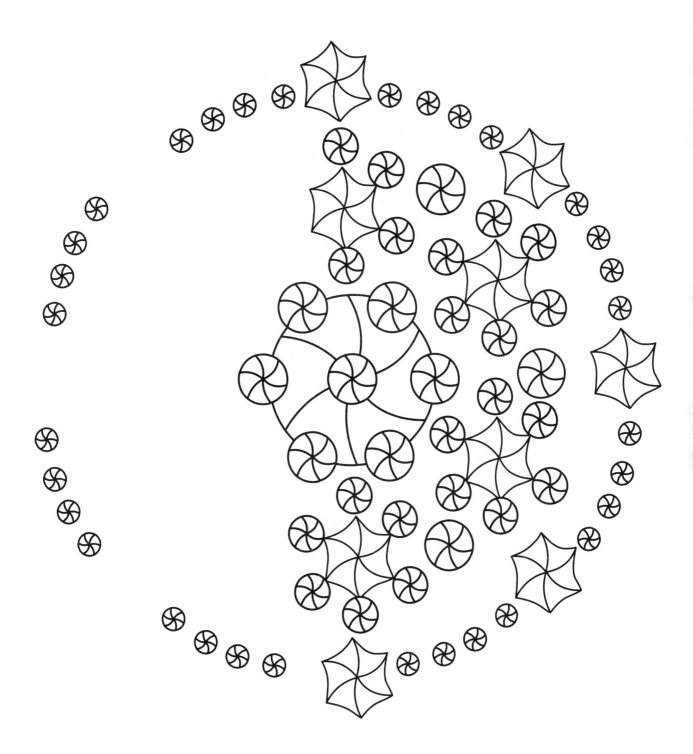

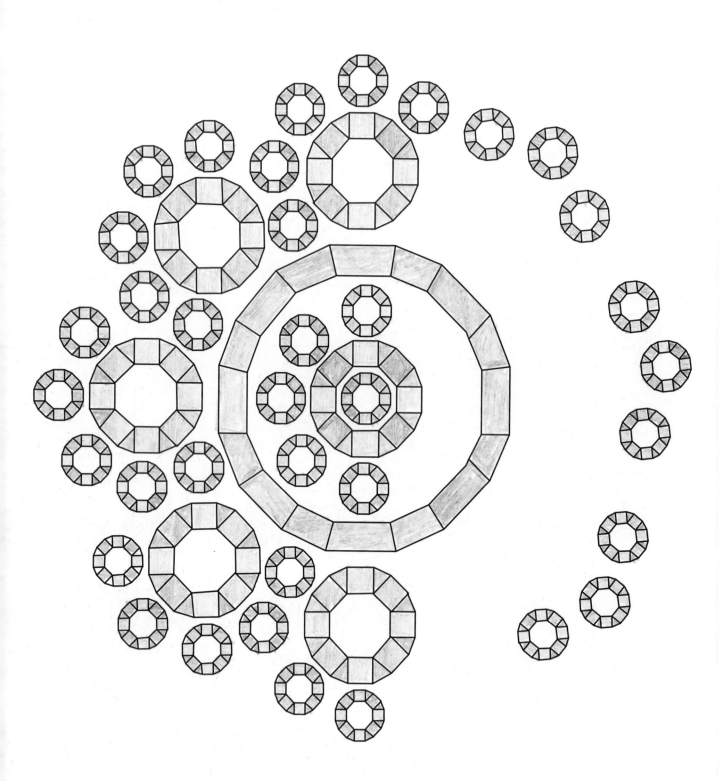

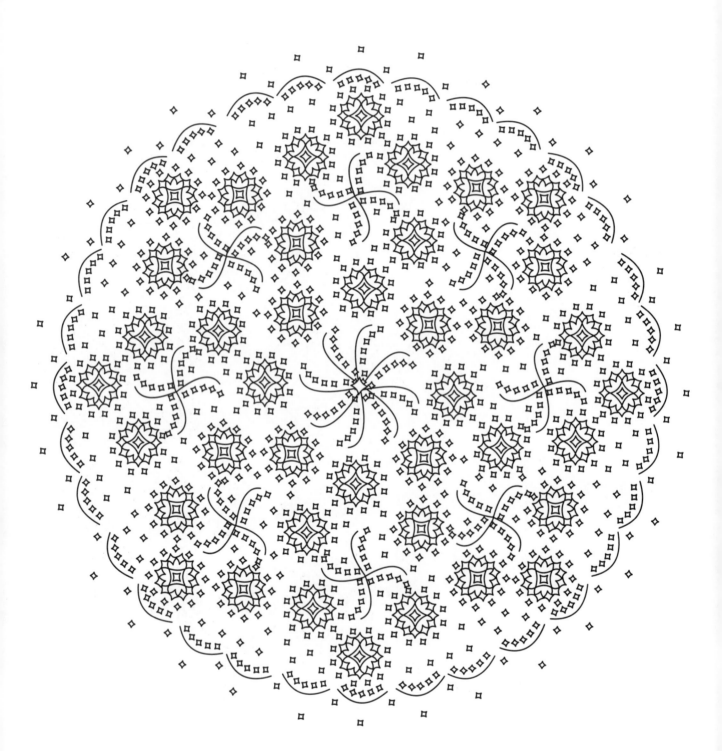

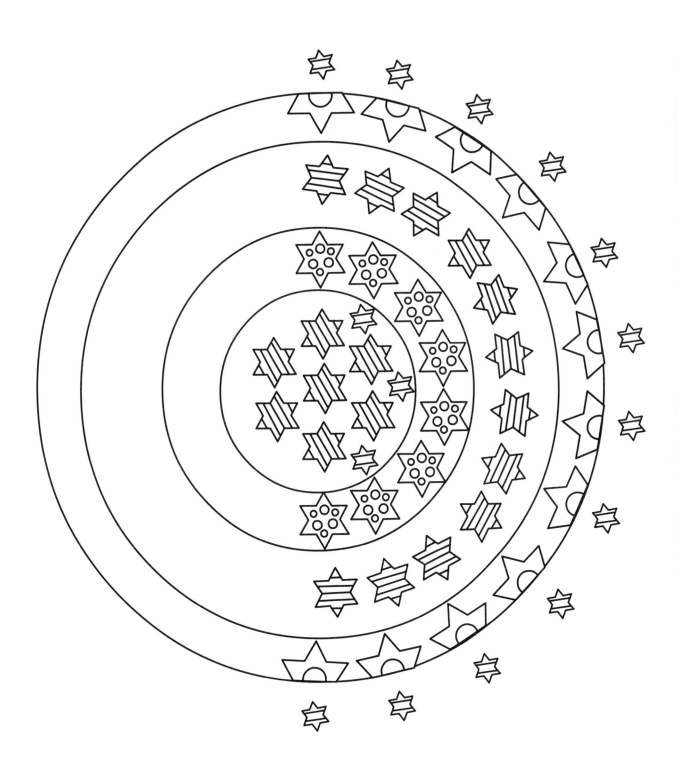

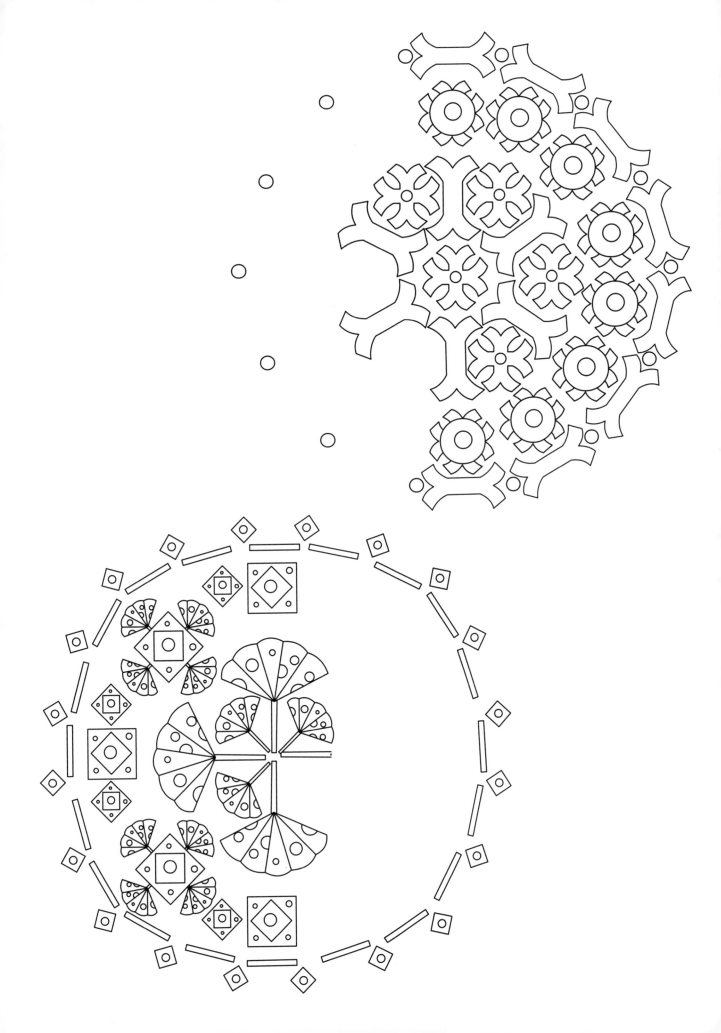

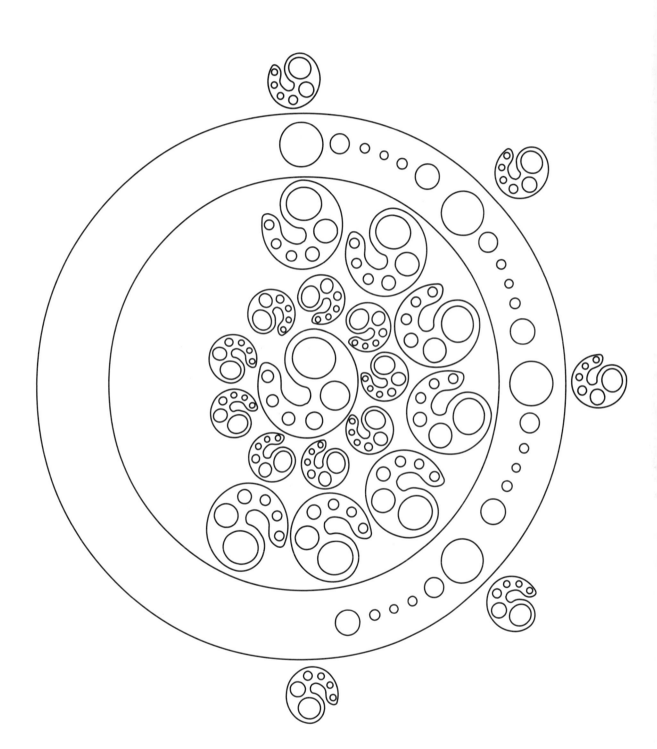

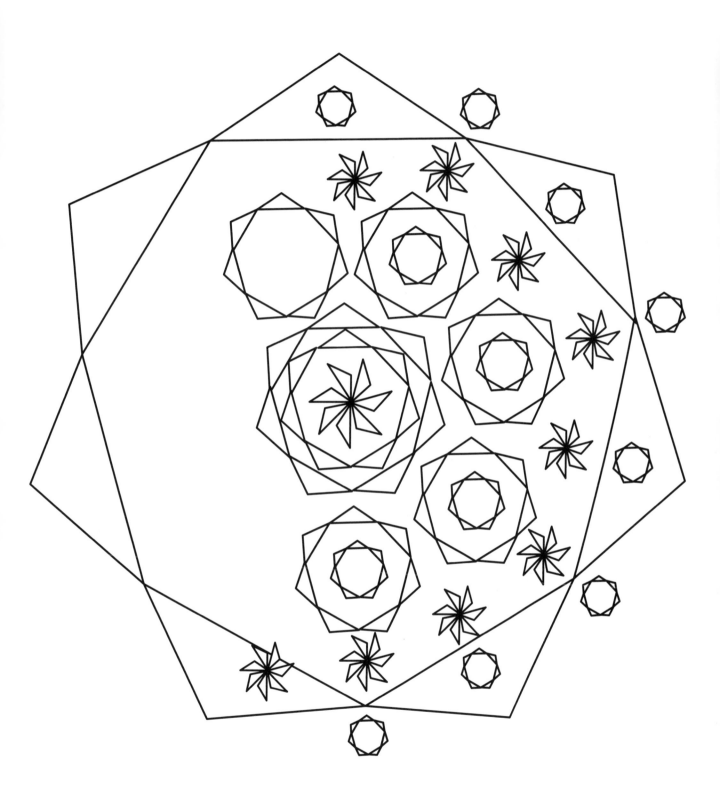

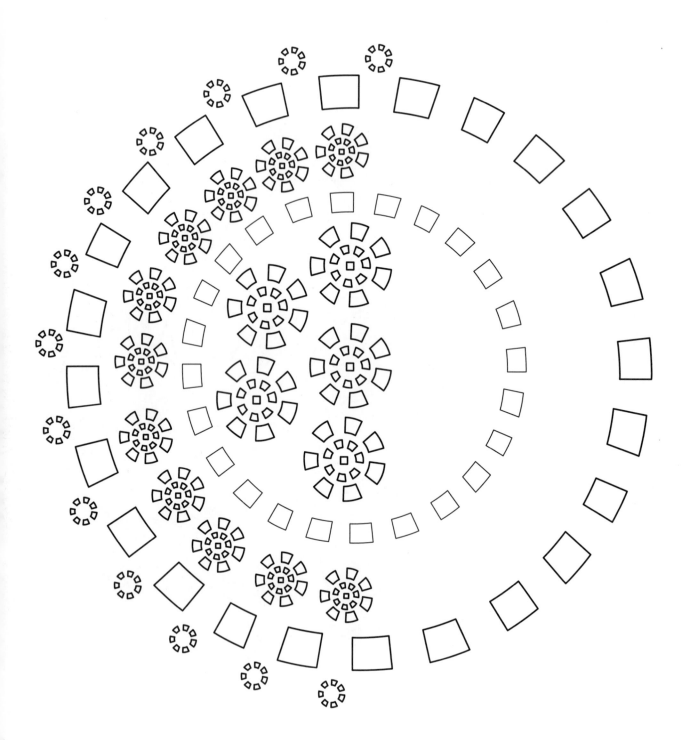

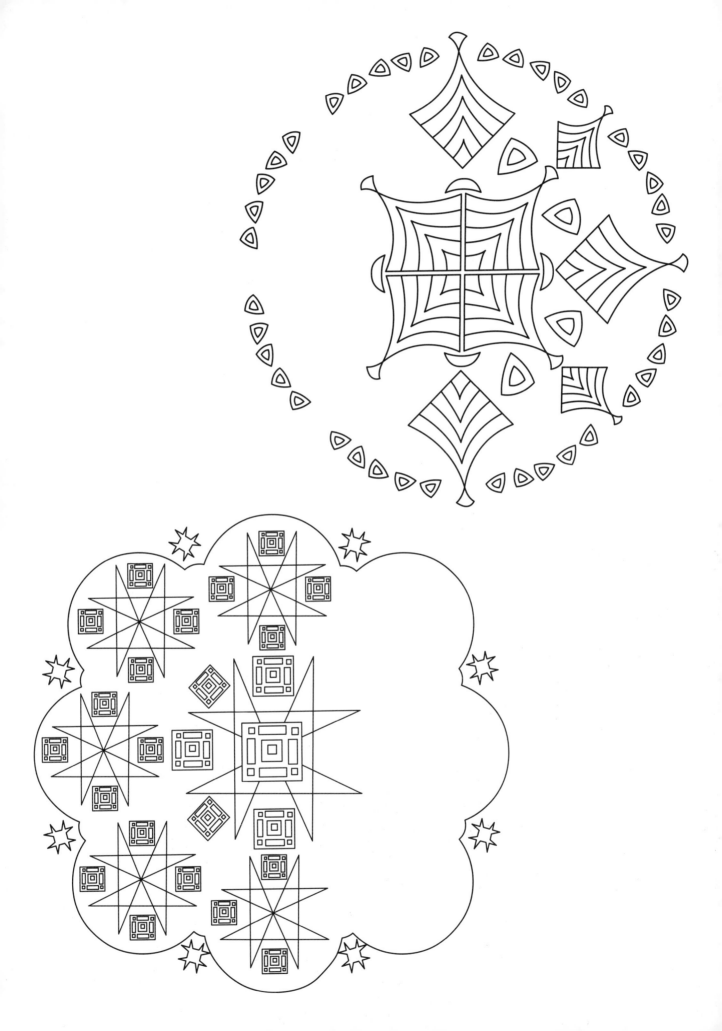

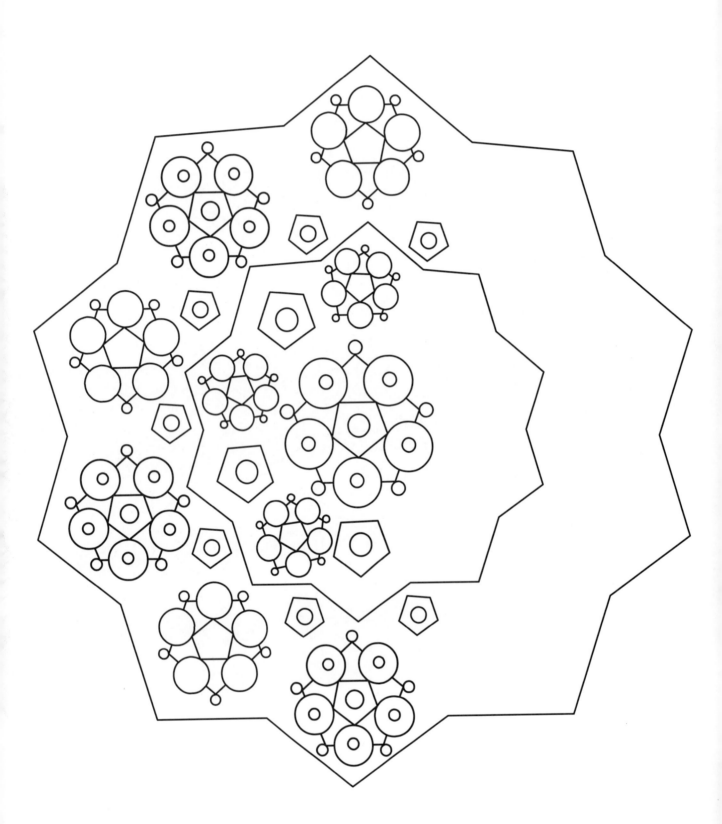

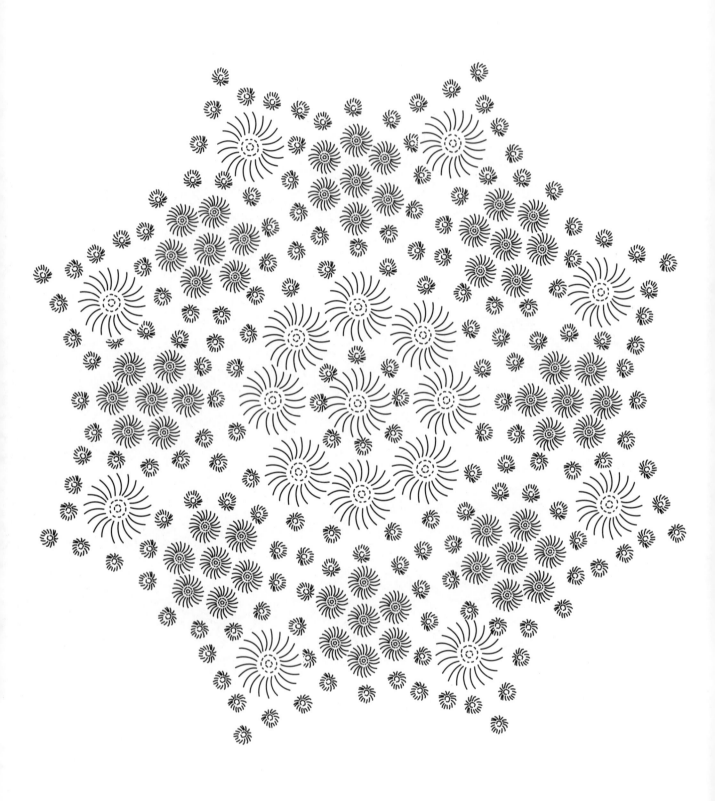

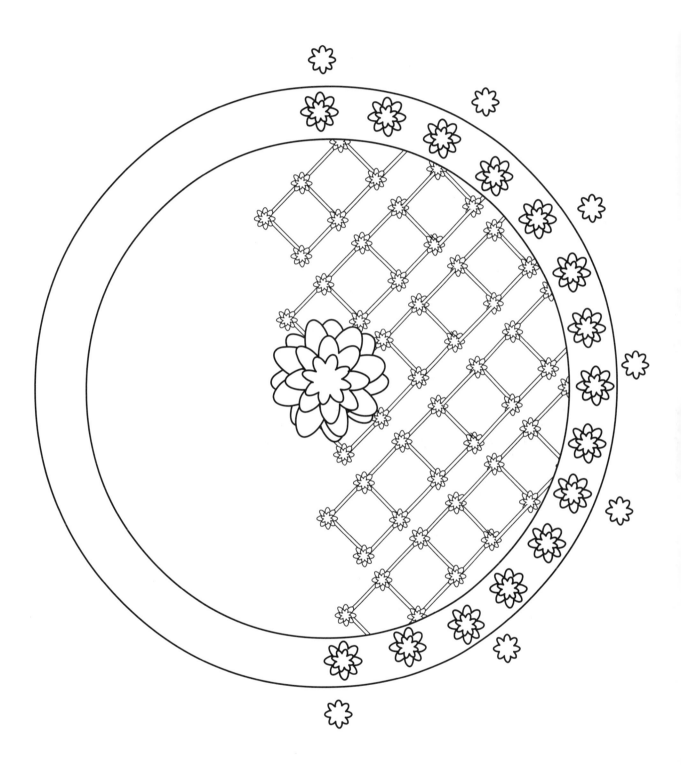

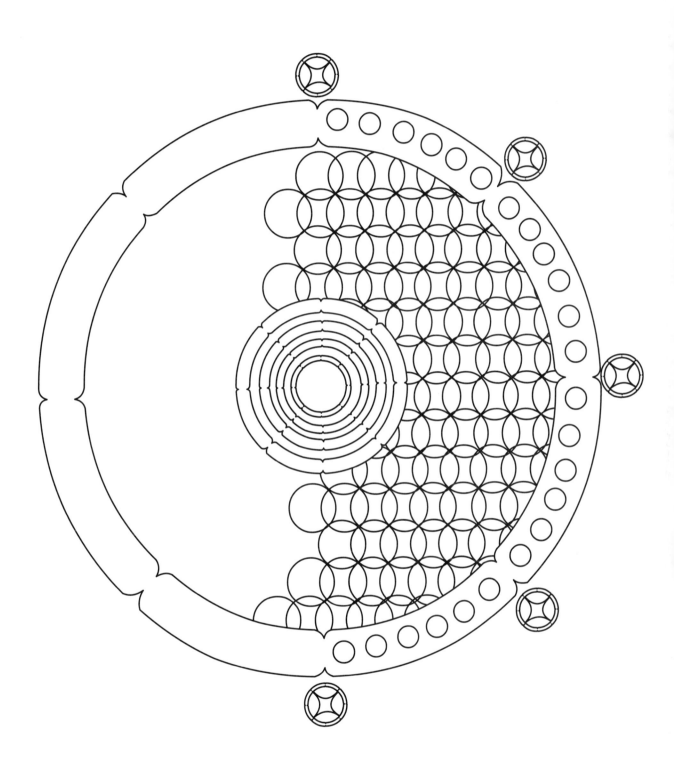

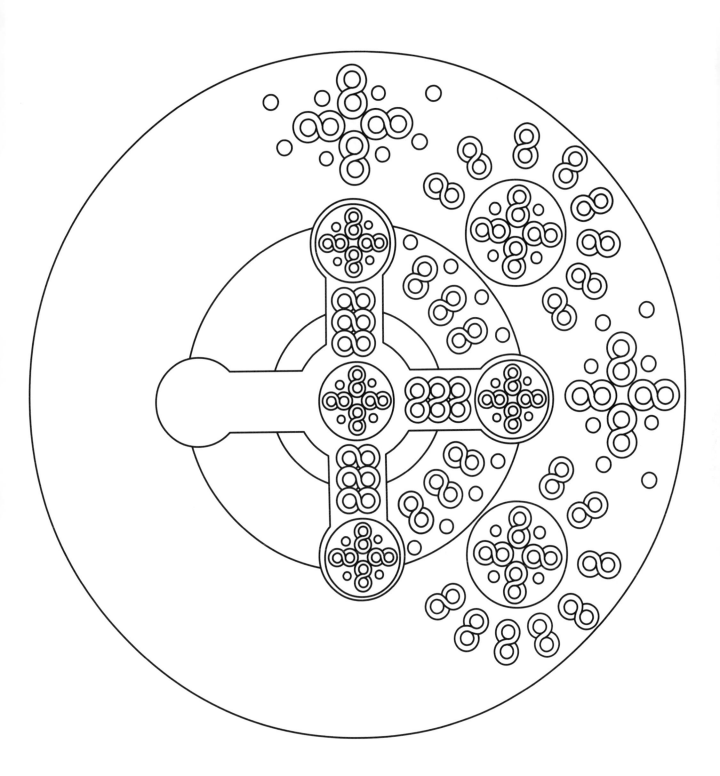

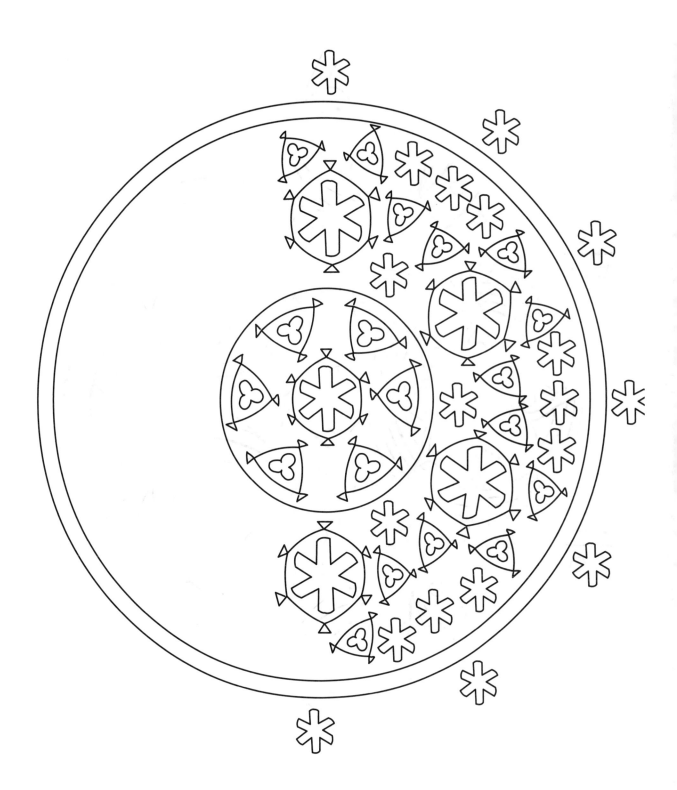

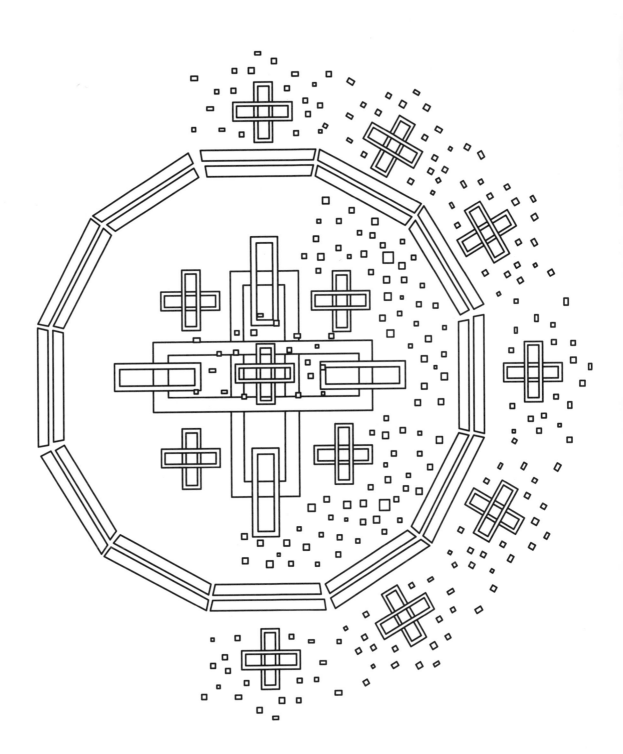